Drug Addiction: Is There Any Hope?

A Biblical Perspective

Murray Miller

Bloomington, IN  Milton Keynes, UK

authorHOUSE®

AuthorHouse™
1663 Liberty Drive, Suite 200
Bloomington, IN 47403
www.authorhouse.com
Phone: 1-800-839-8640

AuthorHouse™ UK Ltd.
500 Avebury Boulevard
Central Milton Keynes, MK9 2BE
www.authorhouse.co.uk
Phone: 08001974150

First published by AuthorHouse   1/15/2007

ISBN: 978-1-4259-2117-0 (sc)

Library of Congress Control Number: 2006910052

Printed in the United States of America
Bloomington, Indiana

This book is printed on acid-free paper.

DEDICATION

To all who – are bound by the addiction of illegal drug use and

desire

more than anything to obtain total freedom from drug use or

distribution. Or if you have considered giving up on life due to

drug addiction, this book is for you.

"And ye shall know the truth, and

the truth shall make you free."

(St. John 8:32)

To all who – have family members or perhaps those who are very

dear

and precious to you who have fallen prey to the illicit drug world.

Please share the information presented in this book with them.

"Bear ye one another's burdens, and

and so fulfill the law of Christ."

(Galatians 6:1)

INTRODUCTION

Hope,

I would like to thank you for choosing to read this book. As you have noticed by its title, the subject is very difficult for many to address and, hopefully, find a promising solution to. Included are a number of easy to follow **principles** to serve as guides in the liberation process of those who appear to be hopelessly entangled within the confines of the illicit drug world. The **principles** mentioned are foundational truths that all referenced materials are based upon. In *Drug Addiction: Is There Any Hope*, I will discuss the **truth** of the *cause, effect,* and *cure* of drug use or solicitation from the biblical, chemical, and anatomical perspectives. However, the primary justifications are biblical.

Although the efforts of substance abuse agencies and comparable organizations are progressing well, it is strikingly noticeable that many of the participants are losing the battle with the illicit drug world. As a result, many participants suffer defeat and become repeat or lifelong abusers. When most people who suffer and experience defeat in life, it is usually due to a lack of *knowledge.* Although many are divided on life's issues, there is something that most of us can agree upon: the unique correlation of *information, knowledge* and *confidence.* The more *information* we have, the more *knowledge* we gain and the more *confident* we become. Once accurate information has been made available and has been properly applied, many who are confined by the illicit drug world can once again become productive citizens, and society will begin to experience the long-awaited relief of the burdensome revolving door syndrome in both correctional and rehabilitation institutions. Applicable exposure to precise information, I believe, will not only guide individuals once again to the junction in life's road, but will also empower them to choose the morally correct path. It is my prayer that you will find *Hope* in the information presented and become better equipped to share with someone who may be in a seemingly hopeless state as a result of illegal drug use.

Murray L. Miller

"Now our Lord Jesus Christ himself, and God,
even our Father, which hath loved us, and hath
given us everlasting consolation and good hope
through grace, Comfort your hearts, and stablish
you in every good word and work."
2 Thessalonians 2:16-17

The Cause

The impact of substance abuse has had a devastating fourfold effect on society for a number of years. Those involved usually recognize that they are affected either spiritually, mentally, physically, or financially. Each phase has metastasized like a malignant cancer, devastating families, friends, and the community as a whole. As reported by the local and national news, at least one billion dollars of the federal state budget is allocated annually to repair damages as a result of substance abuse. Furthermore 80-85 percent of those monies are spent in the areas of medical treatment and law enforcement. In addition, only a small percentage of those dollars are actually used for the purpose of rehabilitation. In the aftermath of it all, mankind must understand two facts. First, drug addiction is a process that involves time, and secondly, in order to direct change we must understand the *forces* that govern change. Everyone, I believe, will gracefully accept positive change, especially those who are entangled in the deceitful web of the illicit drug world. With that said, let's begin with the *Biblical* truth of the matter by answering a few questions along the way such as, <u>What are drugs</u>, <u>where did drugs originate</u>, and <u>*who* or *what* is the cause of drug addiction?</u> In St. John 10:10, Jesus makes a profound statement to mankind.

St. John 10:10

10. The thief [Satan] cometh not, but for to steal, and to kill, and to destroy: I am come that they might have life, and that they might have it more abundantly.

Here, Jesus is informing the world that Satan's chief business is to **destroy** (to tear down and bring to complete ruin). Throughout each generation, the question has remained: Why does Satan desire to deceive and destroy mankind? Starting at the beginning, in Genesis 1:26-27 we learn that God created man in *his own image and likeness.*

Genesis 1:26-27

26. And God said, Let us make man in our image, after our likeness: and let them have dominion over the fish of the sea, and over the fowl of the air, and over the cattle, and over all the earth, and over every creeping thing that

creepeth upon the earth.

27. So God created man in his own image, in the image of God created he him: male and female created he them.

Man, according to the Bible, was created in the image of God. The word *image* comes from the Hebrew word *tselem*, which means shade, shadow, or likeness. Man resembles God in certain respects *without* being equal to him. Man's likeness to God is what truly distinguishes him from the rest of creation. In other words, man is the summit or crown of God's creation on Earth. Therefore, whenever Satan and his demonic host look at man, they are reminded of our creator, the Almighty God. I am not suggesting that man is a god; nor am I suggesting that God is a man. I am just simply stating that man is made after God's own image or likeness. God said, "let us make man in our image, after our likeness." The "us" God was referring to is known as the Godhead: Father, Son, and Holy Spirit. Not three gods, but *one* God revealed in three separate and distinct beings known as the Godhead (Acts 17:29; Romans 1:20; Colossians 2:8-9). Jesus, speaking to the Samaritan woman, said, "God is a Spirit" (St. John 4:24). Man is actually a spirit, has a soul (mind, emotions, and desires), and lives in a body. The Apostle Paul wrote "and I pray God your whole spirit and soul and body be preserved blameless unto the coming of our Lord Jesus Christ" (1 Thessalonians 5:23). The body is the house or tabernacle of both the spirit and soul. We live on a planet made of physical substance; therefore, we must possess a physical body or house to be productive on the planet Earth. The Apostle Paul also wrote:

2 Corinthians 5:1

1.For we know that if our earthly house of *this* tabernacle were dissolved, we have a building of God, an house not made with hands, eternal in the heavens.

When the Apostle Paul said "our earthly house of *this* tabernacle," he was referring to the physical dwelling place of the spirit and soul. This physical dwelling place, which is made of the earth, is what is known as the human body.

In St. Luke 16:19-31, Jesus spoke of two men, one a rich man and the other a beggar named Lazarus. We will begin reading at verse 22:

22. And it came to pass, that the beggar died, and was carried by the angels into Abraham's bosom: the rich man also died, and was buried.

23. And in hell he lifted up his eyes, being in torments, and seeth Abraham afar off, and Lazarus in his bosom.

(Luke 16:19-31 is *not* communicating the message that beggars go to heaven and the rich go to hell.) Please note "Abraham's bosom" was located in paradise and it was where righteous souls were held until the resurrection of Christ (St. Luke 23:43; Ephesians 4:8-10). Both of the men died and were buried. Notice something that is very astonishing to mankind. Although their bodies were buried, both men and Abraham were able to recognize one another. Lazarus died and the angels carried to Abraham's bosom his spirit and soul. The rich man died and his spirit and soul went to hell, which was next to or across from Abraham's bosom. I have presented this illustration to furnish proof that your body is an image of your spirit and that your spirit, soul, and body are an image of God. Remember, when Satan looks at mankind he is reminded of the Almighty God.

Next, the question is raised, What propelled Satan to the state that he has such hatred toward God and his creation? One of the answers to this question is found in Isaiah 11:12-15.

Isaiah 14:12-15

12. How art thou fallen from heaven, O Lucifer [Satan], son of the morning! how art thou cut down to the ground, which didst weaken the nations!

13. For thou hast said in thine heart, I will ascend into heaven, I will exalt my throne above the stars of God: I will sit also upon the mount of the congregation, In the sides of the north.

14. I will ascend above the heights of the clouds; I will be like the most High.

15. Yet thou shalt be brought down to hell, to the sides of the pit.

In this passage, one moment Lucifer (Satan) is described as an anointed cherub or angel; next he's an enemy of God. Furthermore, Satan is not only an enemy of God, but he is also man's chief and most vicious enemy. The lessons taught in the Bible are for the sole benefit of mankind, and that is why Jesus informs us that Satan only comes to *steal*, to *kill*, and to *destroy* (St. John 10:10). One of Satan's corruptible schemes is to manipulate the natural resources that were initially placed upon the earth for the benefit of mankind. He accomplishes this by deceiving mankind to twist or alter the intended use of our natural resources, ultimately bringing man to a degree of self-destruction. All of Satan's thoughts, plans, or ideas are deceptive, destructive, and deadly. Satan's motives are driven by the fact that he was cast out of heaven and eternal damnation awaits him. That is why he hates anything created by God, especially those who resemble God, like you and I. It is imperative to note that mankind is a witness to the greatness of God, and more than anything; Satan would like to destroy everything that is a testimony to God's greatness. Take a look around and just envision all of God's creations and know that everything created by God has a divine purpose designed by the creator for mankind.

St. John 1:3

3. All things were made by him: and without him was not anything made that was made.

Here we have John, who was inspired by God, informing humanity that God created everything (all natural resources) on this Earth. Therefore, we must seek God's infinite wisdom concerning the use of these natural resources or materials within the Earth, especially drugs and the chemical components used to produce drugs. There are hundreds of drugs or narcotics that are known to man and we will discuss a few, but first let's define the term *drugs*. The word *drug* is defined as a medicine used for the treatment of disease. When used in this capacity, the intent of a drug is to bring the body into a state of ease often referred to as homeostasis.

The two most common types of drugs we will examine are Narcotics and Hallucinogens

Narcotic – is referred to as an addictive drug that reduces pain, alters mood, and usually induces sleep, stupor, or euphoria. (A stupor is a state of reduced sensibility and mental numbness, or being dazed. Euphoria is a feeling of great happiness or well being.)

Hallucinogen – a substance that induces hallucination, a false or distorted perception of objects and/or events with a compelling sense of their reality.

As we see, the word *drug* itself is accompanied by several pros and cons; that is to say, drugs can either be beneficial or harmful, depending upon the use.

A Biblical Examination

Let's examine the Word of God (Bible) and references to narcotics and hallucinogens. We will begin our reading in the book of Galatians:

Galatians 5:16-21

16. *This* I say then, Walk in the Spirit, and ye shall not fulfill the lust of the flesh.

17. For the flesh lusteth against the Spirit, and the Spirit against the flesh: and these are contrary the one to the other: so that ye cannot do the things that ye would.

18. But if ye be led of the Spirit, ye are not under the law.

19. Now the works of the flesh are manifest, which are *these;* Adultery, fornication, uncleanness, lascivious,

20. Idolatry, witchcraft, hatred, variance, emulations, wrath, strife, seditions, heresies,

21. Envyings, murders, drunkenness, revellings, and such like: of the which I tell you before, as I have also told *you* in time past, that they which do such
things shall not inherit the kingdom of God.

From the time of the fall of the human race until the present day, mankind, independent of God, has propelled himself to fulfill the lusts or desires of the flesh (sinful appetites and passions). Adam, who was created perfect, chose to satisfy his fleshly appetite and disobey God by partaking of the fruit from the tree of knowledge of good and evil (Genesis 2:17). And as a result of Adam's partaking of the tree of knowledge of good and evil, an inward desire to fulfill the lusts of the flesh, which are manifest in "works," was passed on to the entire human race.

In verses 19-21, there are seventeen works of the flesh, or sins, that are mentioned. Another verse pertinent to this point is Revelation 21:8

Revelation 21:8 states

8. But the fearful, and unbelieving, and the abominable, and murderers, and whoremongers, and sorcerers, and idolaters, and all liars, shall have their part in the lake, which burneth with fire and brimstone: which is the second death.

The work of the flesh that we will study is the sin of **witchcraft** spoken of in verse 20 of Galatians chapter 5. *Witchcraft* is derived from the Greek word *pharmakeia,* which is pronounced "far-mak-i'-ah." The term *sorcerers,* in Revelation 21:8, is derived from the Greek word *pharmakeusin.* The pronunciation of the word *pharmakeusin* is "far-mak-yoos-in." The words *witchcraft* and *sorcerers* can both be defined as those who use drugs for the purpose of mind- or mood-altering effects; to charm, to induce a state of enchantment, or to be under the power of enchantment for the purpose of producing supernatural effects in one's own life or the lives of other people. *Supernatural effect* is a term that refers to occurrences or behaviors that are outside of the natural realm. In other words, getting high, which is actually slang for an intoxicated or euphoric condition, is synonymous to supernatural effects. For this purpose of this text, the phrase "one's own life" refers to individuals who are substance abusers or drug addicts. In addition, when the definition mentions "the lives of other people," it is referring to the individuals known as drug suppliers, who are commonly known as pushers or dealers. It is important to note that knowledge of the truth about anything resides in insight into its origin or its roots. Witchcraft and sorcery, commonly known as illegal drug activity or substance abuse, is one of many methods Satan uses to lure mankind into a state of self-destruction.

When researching drugs such as cocaine, we learn that it is a narcotic alkaloid extracted from the coca leaf. Coca is an Andean evergreen shrub; its leaves contain cocaine. God's purpose for creating the coca leaf was divine and not destructive in nature, which is the case with the illegal usage of the extracts from the leaf. Derivatives of the coca leaf remain beneficial in the medical arena. The two most popular uses of cocaine are as anesthetics or analgesics. An anesthetic is a drug that produces anesthesia, which is a loss of sensation with or without a loss of consciousness. Anesthetics are commonly used by licensed anesthesiologists within hospitals and medical facilities throughout the world. An analgesic is a drug that reduces or eliminates pain throughout the body.

In Genesis 2:7 the bible states:

Genesis 2:7

7. And the Lord God formed man of the dust of the ground [earth], and God breathed into his nostrils the breath of life; and man became a living soul.

From the teachings of this passage, we understand that God formed man from "the dust of the ground." How astonishing it is to know that a vast majority of medications prescribed by physicians, as well as those that are sold in local pharmacies, are derived from ingredients that are made of chemical compounds found in the Earth. Moreover, God, in his infinite wisdom, placed chemicals that are formed into medicines on the Earth to treat our bodies, which were made from the earth, or "the dust of the ground." As stated earlier, every resource upon this Earth has a divine purpose, and we must seek the wisdom of God to achieve the maximum benefit of each resource. If we do not adhere to the divine plan of God, we are defenseless against Satan's deceitful and destructive plans.

Satan, the Prince of This World

Satan is the adversary of everything that is good, including all things created for the benefit of mankind. When the Bible tells us that Satan is the *prince* of the world, it is simply conveying the message that Satan is the ruler of lawlessness and life with the absence of God's guidance. The word *prince* comes from the Greek word *archo*, which means magistrate, prince, or ruler. "Satan rules in the sphere where the inhabitants of the world's system live a life of rebellion based on the godless condition of humanity, which constitutes the only seat or throne of his authority" (W. E. Vines) . A very common method used by Satan to lure a person into spiritual, mental, and physical bondage (which is the result of illicit drug use) is to tempt the person with something that appears to be satisfying, and in the end, deceive the individual into using the benefits of God in a way that is the opposite of God's natural purpose or plan. The aforementioned is more simply known as temptation. The book of James states:

James 1:13

13. Let no man say when he is tempted, I am tempted of God: for God cannot be tempted with evil, neither tempteth he any man:

James says, "God cannot be tempted with evil, neither tempteth he any man." Illicit drug use is evil by nature and practice. It causes man to enter into a state of gradual deterioration, which afflicts him spiritually, mentally, physically, and financially.

Understand, Satan portrays sinful pleasure and moral wickedness as an innocent or harmless act, however, throughout the Bible each book depicts one person after the next warning mankind of Satan and his devices. Let's read what a few of them have to say. We will begin with Jesus Christ:

Jesus Christ

St. John 14:30

30. Hereafter I will not talk much with you: for the prince of this world cometh, and hath nothing in me.

When Jesus said "the prince of this world cometh, and hath nothing in me," he was simply conveying the message that there is no way possible that his nature and the nature of Satan could ever be synonymous. Remember, Jesus said that his assignment was to bring *life* in the abundance thereof, and the mission of Satan was to *steal, kill,* and *destroy* life or lives (St. John 10:10).

Apostle Paul

2 Corinthians 4:3-4

3. But if our gospel [good news] be hid, it is hid to them that are lost:

4. In whom the god [Satan] of this world hath blinded the minds of them   which believe not, lest the light of the glorious gospel of Christ, who is the image of God [the God of all Creation] should shine unto them.

Blinding the minds of "them which believe not" refers to non-Christians and the individual who would normally live his life under the power of sin and Satan. Yes, Satan is usually successful at blinding minds (distorting the true perception of a situation) by manipulation and deceptive reasoning. For example, Satan will deceive people into believing they can seemingly escape the pressures of life by practicing drug use. Or Satan will deceive people into believing they will not be accepted as part of the "in crowd" if they do not engage in a lifestyle that's saturated with illicit drug use. Truth be told, what people are actually missing is the **light** of the glorious **gospel** of **Christ** being shone upon them, which will transform a lost and depraved life into one that is full of hope and foresight. Using drugs to hopefully fill a void in one's life is a very common method used by Satan to cause people to fall prey to his life-altering devices. Furthermore, once the individual has fallen prey to the wiles designed by Satan, life seemingly becomes more difficult to bear. However, it is important to remember there is only *one* true answer to all of the problems that man will face in life here on Earth, and it is found in the Word of God. Satan will always present a false sense of hope by trying to lure man into putting trust in people or things, though the only hope for man resides in God's divine plan for man. Another passage that exposes the plan of Satan is found in the book of Ephesians.

Ephesians 6:12

12. For we wrestle [war] not against flesh and blood, but against principalities, against powers, against the rulers of darkness of this world, against spiritual wickedness in high places.

In this passage, the message conveyed by the Apostle Paul is that man's battle is actually not with mankind. Understand, I am not implying that situations do not arise when disagreements occur between individuals; I am simply stating that our ultimate battle is spiritual in nature and the enemies are Satan and his regime. When Paul states that we war against the "rulers of darkness of this world," he is referring to the spiritual rebels who rule darkness, which is emblematic of all sins known and unknown, all wickedness, and all spiritual depravity upon the Earth. As stated earlier, illicit drug use for the purpose of enjoyment is an act of sin that alters an individual's mental faculties. The Bible refers to drug use as sin in the form of witchcraft or sorcery. More specifically, once people engage in such activity, they are entering into an arena that is saturated with a host of demonic spirits that rule in that arena. Therefore, there is no way possible for the outcome to be representative of victorious and wholesome living. We will expound upon this concept in greater detail later. Let's take a minute to examine what the Apostle Peter has to say concerning the destructive scheme of Satan.

1 Peter 5:8

8. Be sober, be vigilant; because your adversary the devil, as a roaring lion, walketh about, seeking whom he may devour:

Here we see a message written primarily to Christians describing how Satan is able to enter in and destroy mankind. 1 Peter 5:8 warns the believer of being *sober*, which means to have a complete and undisturbed understanding of known and unknown dangers or snares that lurk around on a daily basis. The term *vigilant*, as stated in this verse, means to live a life that represents an attitude of moral alertness, devoid of anything that would obscure the truth. We understand from scripture that Satan is man's chief adversary or contender, but the way or manner in which he appears makes him most detrimental to mankind. When Satan comes as a roaring lion, the Bible is alerting us that Satan is one who possesses a violent and explosive nature, a nature that can only lash out and devour individuals who do not have the *power* to detect and resist him. The power that I am referring to, which discerns what's life or death, is found in the knowledge of Jesus Christ, our Lord and Savior. By empowering yourself with Biblical knowledge, you are better equipped to understand the following statement: We were at war long before individuals such as Sadaam Hussein, Osama Bin Laden, and Adolph Hitler ever came onto the scene; this war is and has always been with Satan and his army of demonic spirits, who roam the realms of the Earth. These demonic forces have been here since the fall of man (Adam and Eve). However, in order for these demonic forces to be successful in destroying mankind, they must distort the mindset or take possession in the body of a life form such as mankind. St. Luke states:

St. Luke 11:24-26

24. When the unclean spirit [demon] is gone out of man, he walketh through dry places seeking rest; and finding none, he saith, I will return unto my house whence I came out.

25. And when he cometh, he findeth *it* swept and garnished.

26. Then goeth he, and taketh to *him* seven others spirits [demons] more wicked than himself; and they [demonic spirits] enter in, and dwell there: and the last state of that man is worst than the first.

This depiction refers to an individual whose life is in a sin-driven state. However, demons cannot take up residence in a house or body that belongs to or has been committed to God. I am not stating that Christians are exempt from the temptations of demonic spirits; I am merely stating that Christians are spiritually prepared to withstand the wiles (schemes) of the world's system, which most often lead to a life of transgression or practicing sin. We must be wise to the fact that witchcraft and sorcery both open the door to a type of bondage that's violent and destructive in nature. This bondage reveals itself in the form of illegal drug use and addiction, drug trafficking, and substance abuse.

Finally, the root cause of drug use and solicitation is not man but Satan. Man, devoid of spiritual and moral insight, is merely an instrument used and manipulated by Satan to carry out his primary mission, which is to steal, kill, and destroy. Satan is usually successful at achieving his goal by altering what's *good* and annihilating mankind with the good that has been altered.

The Effect

To date, millions of precious lives have been left in ruins as a result of substance abuse and drug trafficking. The impact is felt both directly and indirectly. For example, think of the implication in relation to a child whose parent or maybe both parents are substance abusers. The effects cascade into a whole gamut of additional implications that affect an entirely different generation, ultimately debilitating an entire family spiritually, mentally, physically, and financially—thus the fourfold effect.

Please understand, when an individual is tempted to sin, resisting may seem difficult, because the individual offers no weapon of defense against the temptation to abuse drugs. However, once an individual becomes a born-again Christian, God and his infinite Word is his weapon of defense, and he has God's assurance that God will keep him during all temptations, great and small. In 1 Corinthians 10:13 we find:

1 Corinthians 10:13

13. There hath no temptation taken [laid hold on] you but such as is common to man: but God who is faithful, who will not suffer [allow] you to be tempted above that ye are able [beyond your ability to resist]: but will with the temptation make a way to escape, that ye may be able to bear it.

As we can see, God has made a promise to keep those who are born-again in the midst of temptation by providing a way of *escape*. The way of *escape* is an in-depth knowledge of God's Word and an invaluable relationship with him. Paul said, "there hath on temptation taken you." In other words, nothing will capture you by surprise. The Bible will uncover and make you aware of all temptations known to man. The temptations of Satan are evil in nature, and their sole purpose is to cause mankind to fall into a state of mental and physical bondage. Whether you're a Christian or not, Satan's temptations expose weaknesses in people, and as a result, the effect of yielding to temptations will manifest in the lives of those who have fallen prey. There is hope, so don't worry. We read earlier that "all things were made by God; and without Him was not anything made" (St. John 1:3). Again, God created the Earth and all of the natural resources, as well as chemicals found therein. However, he does not approve of substance abuse and the distribution of drugs for the purpose of illegal profit.

What are some of the effects of drugs such as cocaine and marijuana? Initially, the individual experiences excitement or euphoria. This is soon followed by a crash, which is said to be a period of fatigue, anxiety, or depression. The initial symptom associated with the onset of addiction is an acute desire for more of the narcotic to alleviate the affects of the crash. Both cocaine and marijuana can impair an individual's motor response of the brain and contribute to a number of DWI related accidents and deaths. Users of marijuana and other hallucinogenic drugs often experience flashbacks, or unwanted recurrences of a drug's effects weeks or months following usage. At this point, usage has elevated to a level that's habitual, and abstaining from most of these drugs will result in some form of withdrawal that can be life-threatening. However, with continued use of any addictive drug, tolerance develops, which perpetuates to a higher level of dependency in hopes of achieving the same level of gratification that was initially experienced. Some drug users prefer intravenous transmission, which results in the sharing of hypodermic needles, imposing a greater risk of contracting AIDS, hepatitis, and various forms of other opportunistic disease. In addition, unhealthy behaviors such as increased promiscuity and prostitution are classic characteristics that pose an even greater threat to an individual's livelihood. Illegal drug activity is risky business with a cost not imposed by God but by Satan and the choices of mankind. An additional health hazard is the purity of these substances. Drug overdose, as reported by the local and national news, has become a serious problem today and is responsible for numerous deaths each year. Additional criminal behaviors, such as theft and prostitution, are no stranger to many drug users. The aforementioned are just two of many means most users employ to support their maladaptive lifestyle. The user's preoccupation with supplying his or her habit, coupled with the altered effects it has on one's emotional state, will ultimately destroy the individual's ability to financially support his or her family, due to insubordination of workplace policies and statutes. Codependency is another concern in relation to family dynamics, as issues of trust surface in relation to time management and the mismanagement of funds necessary for meeting the basic needs of the family. During the early 2000s, the United States experienced an increase in the number of pregnant women incarcerated who had high-risk births associated with drug use (Department of Health and Human Services). Typically these infants have a higher rate of mental, physical, and social dysfunctions, which can result in unwanted hardships and even death. Pregnant women who contact the AIDS virus through intravenous drug use stand a great chance of passing the virus to their unborn infants. Quite often, the question is raised, How can a person be deceived into using drugs; moreover, what leads a person to experiment with illegal drugs? Since we understand that it is not God who tempts man with drug use, let's finish reading what James wrote on the subject of being tempted.

James 1:14-15

14.But every man is tempted, when he is drawn away of his own lust [evil desires], and enticed [seduced; deceived].

15. Then when lust hath conceived, it bringeth forth sin: and sin, when it is finished, bringeth forth death.

James says, "when lust hath conceived, it bringeth forth sin." When people's desires are evil and they are totally consumed with the imaginable pleasures of the temptation, a chastely door in their lives is opened and allows sin to have a right to reign in their lives. James also states, "and sin, when it is finished, bringeth forth death." Sin means violating a religious or moral law. After sin has run its course, which is very swift, *death* is the verdict. In Biblical terminology, the term *death* is used interchangeably to mean both physical and spiritual death. The term *death* used in James 1:15 is spiritual in nature and is synonymous with being separated from God. When people are spiritually separated from God, there is no comforter or *helper* to warn them of the attacks and temptations of Satan. As most of us have witnessed either in the news or in our communities, physical death often accompanies illegal drug activity. If Satan can keep man separated from God and introduce the thought of hopelessness, then he (Satan) is able to fulfill his primary objective, which is to steal, kill, and destroy (St. John 10:10). As horrific as this may sound, these are only the initial stages for an individual who experiments with illegal drugs.

One of the methods that Satan uses to accomplish this is working in the "children of disobedience," or individuals who live their lives contrary to the will of God.

Ephesians 2:1-3

1.And you hath he quickened [made alive], who were dead in trespasses and sins:

2.Wherein in times past ye walked according to the course of this world, according to the prince of the power of the air, the spirit that now worketh in the children of disobedience:

3.Among whom also we all had our conversation in times past in the lusts of our flesh, fulfilling the desires of the flesh and of the mind; and were by_nature the children of wrath, even as others.

In verse 2, Paul states, "the spirit that now worketh in the children of disobedience." The Apostle Paul is referring to those who are driven by a demonic host and oppose the amiable Word and plan of God. Paul also states, "the children of wrath, even as others." The "children of wrath" denotes a characteristic relationship of those who are estranged from God with the characteristics of an immorally passionate and violent lifestyle. Satan works through these individuals to manufacture and distribute illegal drugs and ultimately rendering them under the influence when drugs are used for illegal purposes. Please remember, Satan is the tempter!

Cocaine, Presented by the Deceiver of the World – Satan

When cocaine is used in powder form, an individual will usually experience euphoria, which is a feeling of extreme pleasure. This term *euphoria* is synonymous with the terms *blasted* and *high*. Often individuals experience a sense of grandiosity or great power, which in realty is a dangerous state of false perception. Cocaine induced in the form of crack (free-base) yields a potentially life-threatening rush that is short-lived. Furthermore it is followed by a crash, or in other words, a state of depression. Basically crack yields a higher high and a faster fall. Cocaine speeds up the brain and body and also attacks the immune system. The immune system's function is to keep the body from getting sick and serve as an aid to help fight infections or illnesses. The external symptoms that accompany cocaine use include glassy eyes, nasal drainage, profuse sweating, cold chills, dilated pupils, and auditory and visual hallucinations, to name a few.

Cocaine – Chemical Composition

There are three chemicals that form cocaine. They are hydrogen, chlorine, and nitrogen. Please note that nitrogen is a base that the other two chemicals are built upon. For example, when building a house, the foundation is the basis on which the rest of the structure is built upon. Therefore, what we know as cocaine is actually called cocaine hydrochloride.

How does Satan alter or change Cocaine?

When cocaine is cut or broken down, the hydrogen and chlorine are both separated from the nitrogen base. After the separation has taken place, the substance hardens into a solid form called rocks. These rocks or stones are usually broken or cracked into pieces, hence the term *crack cocaine*. The remaining product, the nitrogenous component, is a form of free-base that involves the nitrogen base being freed from the two chemicals previously mentioned (hydrogen and chlorine), resulting in a more potent chemical agent.

Satan's Plan to Destroy the Human Body

When crack-cocaine is introduced into the human body, the first telltale sign of addiction is weight lost. Eventually cellular death is initiated. Cellular death has serious implications, especially as it relates to the neurological functioning of the brain. These implications can be permanent and the most devastating.

There is an area in the brain called the hypothalamus, located within the diencephalons; more internally in the hypothalamus is a small bundle of neural tissue called the "pleasure center." The pleasure center is programmed to release chemicals for the purpose of alerting the human body when it is time to eat and drink, and it also creates a desire to procreate. Additional vital functions include maintaining homeostasis of the internal environment. By regulating the heart rate, body temperature, water, electrolyte balance, and sleeping/waking cycle, the hypothalamus plays a major role in regulating both the physical and emotional state of mankind. Chemical agents known as neurotransmitters, such as norepinephrine and dopamine, are released at the neuromuscular junction and are used to initiate communication between critical pathways, such as those involving the brain and skeletal muscles. Norepinephrine is a hormone released by the adrenal medulla in the sympathetic nervous system. Dopamine is another neurotransmitter essential to the normal functioning of the central nervous system, and Parkinson's disease is due to a deficit of this neurotransmitter. After reading the aforementioned functions within the human brain, one can begin to understand the portion of the Bible that says "I will praise thee; for I am fearfully and wonderfully made" (Psalms 139:14). God is to be reverenced for such an astonishing work: the human body. Remember, God gives life and Satan desires death.

The Process of Cocaine Addiction

1.Cocaine first stimulates the pleasure center and exerts pressure until its dry.

2.The cocaine then begins to produce a rush, or high, by blocking the reabsorption of norepinephrine and dopamine.

3.Norepinephrine and dopamine are locked in the "on" position and continue to stimulate again and again, allowing the body to feel their effects over a prolonged period of time.

4.The sensation (rush, high) is accompanied by an increase in heart rate, blood pressure, and sexual appetite.

5.The dopamine continues to be blocked and is eventually washed away, and the brain's supply becomes inadequate to maintain a "normal" mood.

6.The brain cannot produce neural dopamine fast enough to make up for its loss. Therefore, something very devastating occurs: The pleasure circuits begin to dry up.

7. The cocaine user will then become anxious, awkward, worried, and unable to experience "pleasure" without the use of cocaine.

8.Cocaine is needed to experience pleasure, but using it only depletes the supply of neurotransmitters even more. (At this point, addiction and deception are both operating in the user's life, swiftly propelling him into a state of destruction.)

9.Deep depression begins to be established in the user's life.

10.Cocaine addicts tend to lose weight, have trouble sleeping, and develop cardiac and pulmonary abnormalities. Cocaine addicts spend a great deal of time suffering from various illnesses as well.

Let's take a look at some additional drugs that are commonly abused by illicit drug users. I am presenting these drugs, as well as the previous drug, for the sole purpose of enlightenment and deliverance. Jesus said, "And ye shall know the truth, and the truth shall make you free" (St. John 8:31). Note, truth is the opposite of anything that's false, deceitful, or in error.

Heroin

Heroin, *the most addictive drug known to man*, is actually a synthetic form of morphine. Heroin is white and odorless and has similar effects of other drugs, however, the withdrawal is more symptomatic. The symptoms include respiratory distress, convulsions, coma, and possible death. In addition, most heroin users require medical attention to discontinue the use of the drug due to the seriousness of the symptoms of withdrawal. Heroin users also experience frequent battles with constipation, lowered sex drive, and irregular menstrual cycles.

In recent years, the United States has reported an increase in the amount of heroin use. Intranasal heroin abuse has become a common means by which the substance is ingested. The greatest use of heroin in the United States is among college students and both blue- and white-collar workers. As with other illegal drugs, heroin usage is the beginning of long, dark journey that's loaded with a number of unforeseen dangers. Heroin use will not only destroy the physical body; it will destroy the soul (mind, emotions, and will) as well. Please understand that every action has a reverse or opposing action—a reaction. God has a law that we all must make ourselves aware of: the law of sowing and reaping.

Galatians 6:7-8

7. Be not deceived; God is not mocked: for whatsoever a man soweth, that shall he also reap.

8. For he that soweth to his flesh shall of the flesh reap corruption; but he that soweth to the Spirit shall of the Spirit reap life everlasting.

For example, when a farmer sets out to sow seed in the ground, he has a full understanding that every seed will reproduce itself. Heroin and other illegal drugs have the sins of witchcraft and sorcery attached to them. Witchcraft and sorcery, which are deeds of the flesh, will always produce death, both spiritual and premature physical death. The "flesh" is the fleshly or natural appetites of man, which is human nature without the influence of the Spirit of God.

Morphine

Morphine is a very powerful narcotic derived from the alkaloid family, which is classified as base. They are typically bitter to the taste, nitrogenous, and are extracted from opium. They produce physiological as well as psychological effects. Morphine is prescribed as a powerful painkiller and is also used in hospitals as anesthetics and sedatives. The psychological effects include euphoria and apathy. Apathy refers to a lack of interest or concern that can be critical when making life-altering decisions.

Marijuana

Marijuana is a product made from the dried flower clusters and leaves of the cannabis hemp plant. Marijuana is very popular among teenagers due to its accessibility in both the inner city and suburban communities. This particular drug is usually smoked or eaten. A major effect of marijuana is euphoria, which induces a carefree lifestyle. While under the influence of marijuana, most individuals usually experience poor judgment as well. Remember what Jesus Christ said in St. John 10:10: "The thief cometh not, but for to steal, and to kill, and to destroy:

I am come that they might have life, and that they might have it more abundantly." Satan will always come against anything that's good for you. For example, an education is essential to obtaining economic stability in today's society. However, America is experiencing one of the highest dropout rates in history. I am not alluding to the fact that marijuana use is solely responsible for the dropout rate, but it is certainly a contributing factor. When an individual such as a teenager begin to use marijuana, usually he or she will gravitate toward a carefree lifestyle; furthermore, anything representative of an authoritative environment in which order is established (like most academic settings) becomes secondary or bothersome to the teenager. Eventually the student's academic performance declines and the thought of education having no value is introduced. Where or who do you think this type of erroneous thinking came from? That's right. This mindset comes from Satan. Remember, Jesus's desire is for you to have an abundant life. Marijuana use is another example of the many ways Satan achieves his goal of stealing, killing, and destroying. Some of the more common effects of marijuana include impaired memory, delayed reaction time, confusion, inability to fight off colds and flu, low sperm count, and impaired motor function associated with balance and coordination. Also, marijuana smoke contains many cancer-causing chemicals. Other systems affected involve the vital function of organs such as the heart and lungs.

Ecstasy

Ecstasy is a synthetic drug with both hallucinogenic and amphetamine-like characteristics. An amphetamine is used as a central nervous system stimulant. It is chemically similar to another synthetic drug, methamphetamine, which damages brain cells. Ecstasy is also known as XTC, the wonder drug, and club drug. Ecstasy users encounter problems that are similar to those of amphetamine and cocaine users. Some of the effects are an increase in heart rate, faintness, blurred vision, confusion, depression, and paranoia. Ecstasy, as well as other drugs, will allow an individual to experience a high, but there is always a price to pay. With every rise, there is an inevitable fall. Please remember, ecstasy is a stimulant and it is certain to accelerate physiological activity.

The Deception

People who use illegal drugs often notice a desire to use drugs more frequently. During this stage, the body is gradually developing a tolerance to the drug wherein an increased amount of the drug is needed to duplicate the initial effect. Also at this stage, the user is mentally hearing a voice reminding him of the drug's initial effects. The question is, Who is speaking to the user's mind or psyche? The voice the user is hearing is the voice of Satan and his demonic forces. In their cunning ways, Satan and his demonic forces will deceive mankind further by duping people to chase or pursue that which seemingly appeals to the flesh. Witchcraft and sorcery are fruit or deeds of this deception. Remember, anything that is of God will result in what is representative of God's fruit, and that is indicative of life, holiness, and righteousness. In contrast, the fruit of Satan will always result in death and destruction. Another method of deception used by Satan is the love of money.

1 Timothy 6:10

10. For the love of money is the root of all evil [wickedness]: which while   some coveted [desired] after, they have erred [strayed; seduced] from the faith, and pierced themselves through with many sorrows.

In order to capture something or someone, the proper bait must be used. The bait Satan uses to cause an individual to sell drugs is the love of money. The term to describe the character of this particular individual is an avaricious person, or one who has an extreme desire for wealth fueled by greed. Money itself is not evil, but the love of money will introduce people to all sorts of evils. The love of money has caused many people to sin against God and express a strong unwillingness to heed God's instructions in their lives. Money, basically, is on the Earth to serve man, but Satan has deceived man into serving money. Once again, Satan has twisted or altered what God has already considered good into something man is esteeming more than his love for God. Let's examine another passage:

1 Timothy 6:6-7

6. But godliness with contentment is great gain.

7. For we brought nothing into this world, and it is certain we can carry nothing out.

The writer states "godliness with contentment is great gain." In other words, the individual who lives a pious or devout life in addition to pleasing God is great gain. To gain, as most of us know, is simply to acquire or obtain. As some of us may understand, there is nothing wrong with the possession of wealth or riches, as long as it is acquired in an honest and godly manner. We have heard of a number of reasons people use to justify their decisions to sell illegal drugs. We have described drug activity as a form of witchcraft and sorcery. When the defining of the words witchcraft and sorcery, there is a portion that says "in the lives of other people." Those who seek to produce supernatural effects *in the lives of other people* are considered by society to be drug suppliers or dealers. Some may argue "this is the only way I know to make a living." One of life's basic truths says "everything that seems right may not be the right thing to do." The Bible teaches:

Proverbs 16:25

25. There is a way that seemeth right unto a man, but the end thereof are the ways of death.

The easiest person to lie to is oneself. An individual can easily persuade himself that he is doing the right thing, when Satan himself has set up a smoke screen to deceive the individual. The death referred to in Proverbs 16:25 can also be spiritual or physical; usually in the arena of illegal drug sales, it is both. We must remember, whatever is not of God will always result in destruction or death. The majority of people are reared to earn an honest living. However, when greed and the desire to become rich at any cost saturates one's mindset, the idea of *honesty* is soon forgotten. Let's read what the Bible has to say about the person who earns an honest living in contrast to the one who doesn't.

Proverbs 13:11

11.Wealth gotten by vanity shall be diminished: but he that gathereth by labour shall increase.

Vanity is something that is useless or worthless and also has no positive end. When the writer states "he that gathereth by labour shall increase," he is actually saying, "he who collects money by work or employment shall yield much." Some may argue, selling drugs *is* work and it does yield much or gives a great increase. With that notion in mind, let's read from the writings one of God's prophets, Jeremiah.

Jeremiah 17:11

11. As a partridge sitteth on eggs, and hatcheth them not; so he that getteth riches, and not by right, shall leave them in the midst of his days, and at his end shall be a fool.

It is extremely important that the message of this verse is understood. As God speaks through the prophet Jeremiah, "he that getteth riches, and not by right." He is addressing those who accumulate wealth by dishonest means. These people will not only leave the wealth in the midst of their days, but in their latter days they will grow or come to be those who lack the ability to judge or understand things both natural and spiritual. The partridge is known to build an exposed or unprotected nest, and as a result, the nest and the eggs are easily destroyed. This verse is a symbolic teaching of those who obtain wealth unlawfully, which in the end, someone else will ultimately squander. Please understand people do not all of a sudden decide they are going to give up hope of earning an honest living and begin the solicitation of illegal drugs. Satan has to somehow start a chain of events in their lives that will begin to weaken them both mentally and physically. The chain of events can consist of a number of things such as limited life skills, lack of resources, or diverted attention to material possessions, and a willingness to do anything to obtain temporary wealth. However, there is a lurking variable that is most often ignored. This lurking variable is the voice of Satan and his demonic forces enticing the individual while at the same time blinding him or her from the true nature of the consequences involved. The individual is misinformed regarding the choices her or she has embarked upon. Life is full of choices, and we must make proper decisions if our lives are going to be healthy and productive, as God intended. Let's read what Moses wrote in reference to making choices.

Deuteronomy 30:19

19. I call heaven and earth to record this day against you that I have set before you life and death, blessing and cursing: therefore choose life that both thou and thy seed may live:

Since we are free-will beings, God will not force anyone to serve him. However, God loves us so much that he encourages us to choose life as opposed to death. Notice that the Bible states "I have set before you life and death, blessing and cursing." The life referred to is God, who is the conferrer of life and causes one to live or be made alive. Death is separation from God, which allows ruin to enter an individual's life with no inhibitions. We are also presented with the choice of either blessing or cursing. The word *blessing* used here is from the Hebrew word *barakh (ber-aw-kaw)*, which causes one to prosper spiritually, mentally, physically, and financially. The Hebrew word for *cursing* is *qelalah (kel-aw-law)*, which is the lowering to a lesser state in life. Too many mistakes are made simply because people do not make careful, well-thought-out choices in life. Most of us are familiar with the saying, "Life is full of choices. Just be sure to make the right ones." Please remember we are all free to choose any path in life, however, we must be willing to accept the consequences that follow the choices we make. In the Gospel according to Matthew, Jesus Christ spoke of two entirely different paths (gates), and his teachings will expose the consequences of making right and wrong choices.

St. Matthew 7:13-14

13. Enter ye in at the strait gate: for wide is the gate, and broad is the way, that leadeth to destruction, and many there be which go in thereat: 14.Because strait is the gate, and narrow is the way, which leadeth unto life, and few there be that find it.

Jesus begins by admonishing mankind to enter in at the strait gate. Remember, God loves us so much that he encourages us to make decisions that will yield healthy consequences. First, Jesus mentions another gate, which is "wide" and a way that is "broad." The wide and broad way is saturated with every sinful pleasure imaginable to man. Once an individual enters through this gate, his life will eventually decline to a state of destruction and possibly death (physical). One may ask, What is the length of time for destruction and death to manifest themselves in someone's life? The pace at which death and destruction travels can be either swift or slow, but it is sure to occur in the life that enters through the wide gate and travels the broad way. The Bible states "God is not a man that He should lie" (Numbers 23:19). Please remember God is the author of the Bible, and if he has declared that something would come to pass, whatever has been declared will come to pass. The next gate is "strait" and "narrow." The "strait and narrow way" is quite simple. It is a lawful and obedient way, which leads to life in abundance. As earlier mentioned, this is the way Jesus encourages mankind to travel. If you've noticed, each gate has a *way* associated with it. The way is the manner or way of life an individual lives, which can lead to either destruction or life. Once again, we are encouraged by Jesus Christ to choose the strait gate that leads to life. On the contrary, Satan will only present you with one choice: " the wide and broad way" (darkness, depression, destruction, etc.). It doesn't matter what the choice is. If it is presented by Satan, the result is certain to produce death—both spiritual and premature physical death. You see, illegal drug activity has a very devious influence on both the user and the dealer, and in the end, no one wins!

Most of us know of someone, whether directly or indirectly, who has chosen to experiment with illicit drugs. Through the intentional distortion of the truth by Satan, we have witnessed the manifestation of a form of slavery or bondage in their lives. The term *slavery* may seem to be a little harsh, but it's appropriate for the lifestyle. A slave is someone who is abjectly subservient to a specific person, emotion, or influence.

The influence of illicit drug activity has lowered millions of people to a state of forced servitude. The life of an addict or dealer consists of the daily activity of seeking drugs for the sole purpose of the superficial benefits that the drug might yield. For example, if my desire is to control or enslave your life, I would first present you with something that appears to be harmless and seemingly yields a good time, however, during the presentation, I would conceal all signs of depression, destruction, heartache, misery, jail, or death that are sure to accompany my product. This is exactly what Satan does with the temptations of witchcraft and sorcery. By the means of his seductive manner, Satan presents the drug world in such a way that people are blinded to the true effects of illicit drug use. The ultimate effect upon a person's life is that Satan becomes his or her slave master. I understand the term *slave master* may seem to be harsh, but it's reality. A slave master will never have your best interest at heart. Instead, he will very doggedly work a slave until he or she is unable to function. And he would also undress a slave of any identity and self-worth he or she may have. This is very similar to what Satan does to those who are bound by the practice of using or selling illicit drugs. He is successful in achieving this very intense level of control primarily by blinding the minds of those who do not believe (2 Corinthians 4:4). Mankind alone does not possess the ability to conquer Satan and his demonic forces. According to the Bible, the power and ability to achieve victory over Satan only comes by way of Christ Jesus. Once an individual receives Jesus Christ as Lord and Savior, he or she is given authority over all the power of the devil. The Gospel according to Luke states:

Luke 10:19

19. Behold, I [Jesus Christ] **give unto you power to tread on serpents** [demons] **and scorpions** [demons]**, and over all the power of the enemy: and nothing**

shall by any means hurt you. (I will explain in detail later.)

We must remember that the function of an individual demon is not independent of other demonic spirits. Jesus, referring to the unity of Satan's kingdom, said, "Every kingdom divided against itself is brought to desolation; and every city or house divided against itself shall not stand" (Matthew 12:25). For example, there are several manifest lifestyles that will accompany that of illegal drug use, such as adultery, fornication, uncleanness (homosexuality or lesbianism), hatred, strife, envy, murder, lying, theft, and drunkenness (Matthew 15:19, Galatians 5:19-21, Revelation 21:8). Listen to what Jesus said in reference to the conspiring activity of demonic spirits:

St. Luke 11:24-26

24. When the unclean spirit [demon] **is gone out of a man, he walketh through dry places, seeking rest; and finding none, he saith, I will return unto my house whence I came out.**

42

25. And when he [the unclean spirit] **cometh, he findeth it** [the human body] **swept and garnished.**

26. Then goeth he, and taketh to him seven other spirits [demons] **more wicked than himself; and they enter in, and dwell there: and the last state of that man is worst than the first.**

Jesus is indicating that demons not only seek companionship with each other, but are also coworkers in the oppression of an individual's spirit, soul, and body. As horrible as the bondage of witchcraft and sorcery may sound, this is only the beginning of a person who is barreling over life's moral cliff, which is similar to human flesh being consumed by a devouring disease. Please do not abandon your quest for freedom, because there is hope! If you are free, please use the information in this book to encourage someone who is bound by illicit drugs, whether using or selling.

On some level, we all have witnessed the effects of the illegal drug world. Whether by way of the local or national news, or even in our own communities, we have come to understand the devastating effects of this lifestyle. Unfortunately many families have suffered tremendously as a result of illegal drug activity, and countless numbers of young men and women wear the scares of a maladaptive behavior, such as illegal drug activity. Please understand, if we are to properly use what God has placed within the Earth, we must first seek his infinite wisdom and trust him to direct our paths in all areas of our lives. With God, there is righteousness and life; with Satan, there is sin and death. People either stand with God in truth and light, or with Satan in error and darkness. There is no neutral territory!

The Cure

In this section, we will explore biblical and practical solutions to conquering the demonic forces responsible for influencing illegal drug activity. In reference to witchcraft and sorcery, we have exposed the characteristics and operations of these sins. One can attest that the aforementioned sins, when indulged, will forcibly lead one down a road that's morally dark and bitter. While traveling this dark and bitter road, one would soon notice that his or her life is engulfed in a sea of ignorance, or in other words, this is a life devoid of any beneficial knowledge. A life that's devoid of knowledge will further expose an individual to many pains, problems, and sins. The user then realizes the need for something that's very critical—a cure. The *cure* from the illicit drug arena is not a magic potion, but a lifeline that's interwoven with hope, confidence, and wisdom. It is the same lifeline that we have been examining from the beginning: the Bible. Once you have a firm grip of wisdom, confidence, and hope, the power and love of God will lift you out of this sea of darkness and transform your life into one that has a blossoming fourfold effect that will manifest itself spiritually, mentally, physically, and financially. The Bible says, "A wise man will hear, and will increase in learning [knowledge]; and a man of understanding shall attain unto wise counsels." (Proverbs 1:4). A *wise* or *prudent* man realizes the urgency of a much-needed rescue, but recognizes he needs help to exit this dark road that's consumed in ignorance. Please remember, *ignorance is simply possessing a lack of knowledge.*

The *cure* is separated into five subsections that will answer several questions and examine some very important principles. The first subsection is *From Darkness to Light,* in other words, from *bondage* to *freedom.* The second is a brief, in-depth study of a very important Christian principle, *Faith vs. Sight.* The third is a teaching on how those who desire to be free should view themselves, *Changing Your Speech.* The fourth is a continuation of the third, but it focuses mainly on a healthy thought-life, *Reproving Negative Thoughts.* The last, which has helped millions to obtain freedom, is simply *Feasting On The Word Of God.* These very practical principles, if practiced on a daily basis, will bring the much-desired liberation from bondage to freedom in an individual's life.

From Darkness to Light, How?

We will begin by scrutinizing and contrasting *darkness* and *light.* First, let's ask the question, <u>What is the most effective method used to contend with darkness?</u> The answer: <u>Expose the darkness to light for the sole purpose to make visible or uncover the reality or origin of the darkness.</u> For the purpose of this text, we will define the word *darkness* as spiritual or moral darkness, emblematic of sin, and as a condition of moral or spiritual depravity (Matthew 4:12-17; Romans 2:17-20; 1Corinthians 4:5; Ephesians 5:8,11; 1Peter 2:9; 1John 1:6-7). We will also define the word *light* as a symbol of the nature of God (1 John 1:5), and also of the Lord Jesus as the illuminator of men (John 1:4,5,9; John 8:12; John 12:46).

Notice what the Bible says concerning both light and darkness.

St. John 1:4-5

4. In him [Jesus Christ] was life: and the life was the light of men.

5. And the light shineth in darkness: and the darkness comprehended it not.

St. John 3:19

19. And this is the condemnation, that light is come into the world, and men loved darkness rather than light, because their deeds were evil.

Acts 26:18

18. To open their eyes, and to turn them from darkness to light, and from the power of Satan unto God, that they may receive forgiveness of sins, and inheritance [joint-heir] among them which are sanctified by faith that is in me.

2 Corinthians 6:14

14. Be ye not unequally yoked together with unbelievers: for what fellowship hath righteousness with unrighteousness? and what communion [participation] hath light with darkness?

Notice the words *light* and *darkness* and how they are symbolically used throughout the Bible. *Light* is used to depict all of the attributes representative of the abundance of life given to man by God. *Darkness* is used to depict a lifestyle of sin and immorality, governed by Satan himself. The first practical truth we must understand is we are powerless against correcting anything that we are unwilling to confront. To be willing, even if you are wounded, to take a stand against the forces that have held you captive is a proclamation you have taken a major step towards deliverance. Once you purpose in your heart not to listen any longer to the deceitful lies of Satan, freedom will begin to manifest itself beyond your wildest imagination. Just in case you were not aware, you can begin to change your life simply by *speaking* and *believing*. I realize this may sound a little strange or even abnormal, but continue reading and I believe that the previous statement—speaking and believing—will become crystal clear to you. Once you're free from the bondage of witchcraft and sorcery, you can remain free forever! Simply accept the solutions in the Bible that are freely given unto all of us. However, if we are to overcome, we must adhere to the teachings of the one who overcame every possible obstacle known to man, Jesus Christ. In reference to Jesus Christ, the great overcomer, the Bible states:

Hebrews 4:14-16

14. Seeing then that we have a great high priest, that is passed into the heavens, Jesus the Son of God, let us hold fast our profession.

15. For we have not an high priest which cannot be touched with the feelings of our infirmities [*Astheneia,* Greek for weaknesses]; but was in all points tempted like as we are, yet without sin.

When Hebrews 4:15 says, "we have not an high priest which cannot be touched with the feelings of our infirmities." The high priest is Jesus Christ, who is "touched," or expresses compassion and understands all mental and physical weaknesses of mankind. Hebrews 4:15 continues by affirming, "but was in all points tempted like as we are, yet without sin." In all "points" or in comparison with every form of temptation known to man, Jesus was tempted (tried) with solicitation to sin but did not give way to the pressures, forces, or persuasions of the temptations.

16. Let us therefore come [draw near; approach] boldly to the throne of grace, that we may obtain mercy, and find grace to help in time of need.

The privilege of approaching the "throne of grace," which is the place of unmerited and unearned favor and loving kindness, has been made available and can be experienced by the entire human race. However, there is one requirement needed in order to approach the throne of grace, Jesus Christ.

Jesus taught "without me, you can do nothing" (St. John 15:5). The word *nothing* is a reference to the limited abilities of mankind to exhibit a lifestyle conducive of an invisible and inward working with outward characteristics—specifically "temperance," which is self-control of sensual desires (Galatians 5:22-23). Once you have acknowledged that you are in need of help, the next step is to submit to God through his Son, Jesus Christ. Submission to God is being subject or obedient to **ALL** of God's teachings, beginning with the saving of one's soul. To be saved is to be delivered from the power of sin and to receive salvation from God the Almighty. Salvation is spiritual and eternal deliverance, which is granted immediately by God to those who accept his conditions of repentance through faith in the Lord Jesus Christ, in whom alone salvation is obtained.

St. John 14:6

6. Jesus saith unto him, I am the way [the means of access to the Father], the the truth [truth in all its fullness and scope], and the life [abundant and eternal life]: no man cometh unto the Father but by [through] me.

Millions of people seek God on a daily basis, desiring to find peace, strength, hope, and even love. Some seek him in their own way or understanding, while others take the advice of Jesus Christ found in St. John 14:6. According to the Bible, Jesus Christ is the way or method of approaching God, the Creator of all. Once again, people hopelessly exhaust themselves seeking God by trusting in their own finite ways or methods. Jesus also informs mankind that he is "the truth," which is opposite of all falsehood, particularly *other* methods used to try to gain access to God. Jesus Christ is also "the life," which is everything from life abundant to life eternal (I will explain later).

Once an individual has come to God through Jesus Christ, there is a promise given by Christ in St. Luke 10:19 that assures total victory over all demonic forces.

Luke 10:19

19. Behold, I give unto you power to tread upon serpents and scorpions, and over all the power of the enemy: and nothing shall by any means hurt you.

If Satan has tormented and controlled your life with the use of illegal drugs and you have now submitted to God, smile and be encouraged; in addition to a transformation from death to life, an emblem of power has been given to you. Take a closer look at what God has given you through his son Jesus Christ. He has given you **power (*Exousia* in Greek)—the authority or ability to destroy or eradicate the works of Satan in one's own life.** The words *serpents* and *scorpions* are used metaphorically to refer to devils and demons. According to the holy scriptures, Satan and his demonic hosts are chief enemies of mankind; therefore, once a person comes to God by way of Jesus Christ (having been born-again), that person is given power to have complete victory over Satan and all other demonic spirits. Traditionally, people get *saved*, are *born-again*, or *accept Jesus Christ as Lord and Savior* for the comfort of knowing that when they perish they are going to heaven. The promise of heaven (eternal life) is genuine, and Christians should patiently and hopefully live for the transition from Earth to heaven. But there are tons of benefits and blessings usually never experienced that are rightfully theirs to claim. Remember, Jesus declared, "I come that they might have life, and that they might have it more abundantly" (St. John 10:10). Those who receive life will undergo a wallowing fourfold effect—spiritually, mentally, physically, and financially—that is greater than the normal or average standards of living. When an individual is bound by drug addiction or the illegal distribution of drugs, the person is *not* experiencing life in its abundance. The one thing Satan *steals* from these individuals is their freedom, or ability to abstain from the illicit drug world, which induces bondage. Please remember, freedom from all forms of bondage is one of the many benefits of being saved or having been born again.

Once a person accepts Jesus Christ as Lord and Savior, he becomes a spiritual potentate, one who has the power and position to successfully resist the pressures and temptations of demonic spirits. Please remember, the devil only fears God, Jesus Christ, and those who live in Christ (Christians). Therefore, to achieve and maintain victory, it is imperative that those who accept Jesus Christ as Lord and Savior remain in Christ. Many people, in times past and present, have struggled to remain in Christ and have succumbed to the wiles or schemes of Satan. A sure method of remaining in Christ is simply being doers or executers of God's Word, and not mere listeners only.

James 1:22-25 (Amplified Bible)

22. But be ye doers of the Word [obey the message], and not merely listeners to it, betraying yourselves [into deception by reasoning contrary to the Truth].

23. For if anyone only listens to the Word without obeying it and being a doer of it, he is like a man who looks carefully at his [own] natural face in a mirror;

24. For he thoughtfully observes himself, and then goes off and promptly forgets what he was like.

25. But he who looks carefully into the faultless law, the [law] of liberty, and is faithful to it and perseveres in looking into it, being not a heedless listener who forgets but an active doer [who obeys], he shall be blessed in his doing (his life of obedience).

I am speaking directly to those who are bound by drug addiction or illegal drug activity. Listening to an inspiring message on deliverance or merely thinking about liberation may not be enough. Those who are bound must go through a process of purging for deliverance to become reality. I would imagine one could equate the process of purging with that of a person who has fallen off a cliff during a mountain climbing expedition. Physically the person appears to be screaming for help, when along comes a rescuer who throws down a rope to pull him to safety. The victim glances aimlessly at the rope, but the purpose of the rope is forgotten and this poor soul appears to be in a state of hopelessness. It is only when the fallen person takes hold of the rope that he will be pulled to safety, regardless of what the condition appears to be. The process of purging is simply to eradicate or uproot any sin, guilt, corruption, vileness, or defilement. We must hold fast to and never let go of God's promises of deliverance when we are confronted with the innumerable challenges life can and will present. Once again, without Christ we can do nothing. Christ is our source, our life, our strength, and our very present help. Mankind's life must mirror the spiritual (Christian) relationship provided by Christ to exhibit the fruit or results of a victorious life. When an individual places his or her trust in God through Jesus Christ, the person will began to experience life in a way never imagined. If you make the decision to choose the aforementioned, you will become the conqueror instead of the one who is conquered.

Once you have placed your trust in Jesus Christ as Lord and Savior and have begun to live in victory, you must never let your guard down. God has provided scriptural proof of mankind's chief enemy, who does not and will not fight a fair battle. Satan, your adversary, will continue to fight you, but be of good cheer because you have power in Christ Jesus to resist Satan. Your next question might be, How does one resist Satan?

James 4:7

7. Submit yourselves therefore to God. Resist the devil, and he will flee from you.

James, in a very compelling way, requests Christians *submit* (to yield) and *resist* (stand firm against or give no place to), which means to oppose. Submitting to God only makes a very fearless statement that God is your superior, not Satan. After submitting to God and resisting Satan, notice the immediate response or reaction is for Satan to flee. Remember, Satan as well as his demonic forces only flee from Christians who have submitted themselves to God and all of his teachings. As society has proven in a very distinct way, those who are in submission to any of the deceptive schemes of Satan lack the ability to resist him or his devices. This is why it is vitally important to always be prepared to resist him and never be caught off guard. Satan, the ferocious enemy to man, will approach you from time to time in many ways, and simply resisting him is all we are asked to do. The Apostle Peter states:

1 Peter 5:8-9

8. Be sober, be vigilant; because your adversary the devil, as a roaring lion, walketh about, seeking whom he may devour:

9. Whom resist steadfast in the faith, knowing that the same afflictions are accomplished in your brethren that are in the world.

Before Peter informs us of the enemy, he first tells us to be *sober*, which simply means to use sound judgment and make wise decisions in practical and spiritual matters. For example, if an individual knows for a fact that fire burns and is painful to human flesh but proceeds to put his hand into the flame and later asks why he was burned, this individual's ability to make correct choices is faulty. Consequently, this is exactly what happens to millions of people who yield to the temptations of illegal drug activity; eventually they will get burned. Next Peter commands us to be *vigilant*. In order for us to be vigilant, we must live a life that encompasses both spiritual and moral alertness. Those who are alert or able to discern what's right and wrong can detect the presence of danger, and with the help of God are able to escape seen and unforeseen danger. Peter then identifies the devil as our *adversary*, which is one who opposes or antagonizes. Once again, Satan only comes to steal, kill, and to destroy. Think for a moment: If Satan is an adversary to the Christian who, through Jesus Christ, has been given power over him (Luke 10:19), how then can an unbeliever or non-Christian attempt to withstand the attacks of Satan? He also comes as a roaring lion, which is used metaphorically to illustrate the fierceness of his strength and the imminent danger of destruction and death. Notice Satan seeks those who are powerless to withstand his devouring scheme. Once again, we are commanded to resist the devil's temptations and any attacks he may send to enslave one's mind, body, or spirit. We are to resist him by remaining constant or steadfast in *faith* (the victorious, power-producing faith in God and his Son Jesus Christ, which is the most powerful force known to man). Having learned how to be sober and vigilant, begin to see yourself as one who is victorious in all circumstances that were otherwise hindrances to you in life, especially illicit drug use.

Do not waste time worrying about why you are often tempted; Satan's desire is to tempt mankind by solicitation to sin, particularly those of us who have been born again. Due to a lack of *power*, people who are held captive in sin by Satan's enslaving schemes are in no position to fight back or resist (Luke 10:19). Therefore, when and how often the temptations come is a sign that you are either free or on the road to freedom. This also identifies the "roaring lion." Once an individual decides to become a Christian, that person is tempted primarily because he or she has been set free and given power over Satan and all demonic spirits.

You can pass out of darkness into light,
from death into life by allowing Jesus to be Lord of your life.

Faith vs. Sight

Considering the large number of people who hold fast to any type of religious belief, they can be identified by one of the two convictions: those who do not have to physically see something in order to believe in the reality of its existence or those who must have some type of physical evidence of an object or promise in order to believe in its reality. There are hundreds of declarations in the Bible that God has vowed to perform in the lives of mankind, but there is one prerequisite to receiving these promises: *faith*. **Faith means being confident that God will do what he has promised and remaining steadfast to God's promises so as to obtain present and future rewards for worthy behavior.**

For example, in the book of Romans, Paul states:

Romans 10:9

9. That if thou shalt confess with thy mouth the Lord Jesus, and shalt believe in thine heart that God hath raised him from the dead, thou shalt be saved.

When the verse states "thou shalt confess with thy mouth," most of us can agree this is very manageable and requires little effort by the reader. However, when the verse states "and shalt believe in thine heart that God hath raised him from the dead," this requires the use of an ability that many people wrestle or struggle with—*faith*. The hope of salvation alone requires one to believe and wholeheartedly accept the deeds performed by God concerning the resurrection of Christ from the dead. The greatest opposition or resistance to your faith is unbelief and doubt. To obtain the promises of God, one must be able to live or walk by faith, that is, to read it, accept (believe) it, and receive it. Read it, accept it, and receive it. Read it, believe it, and receive it! Notice the words *accept* and *believe* are synonymous. In other words, after you've read the promises of the benefits and blessings in the Bible, the next step is to accept, receive, or *agree* with the conditions that must be met in order to obtain the promises. Once again, the conditions are found in one word: *faith*. This brings us to another verse we must explore that will further enlighten us concerning this discussion. In the Apostle Paul's second epistle to the church at Corinth, he made a very brief but powerful statement.

2 Corinthians 5:7

7. For we walk by faith, not by sight.

Most importantly, we are told we must *walk* or *live* by faith. Another definition of the word *faith* is a condition of trusting what has not manifested itself into physical existence (Hebrews 11:7-16); calling those things that be not as though they were (Romans 4:17); the substance, confidence, and assurance of things not yet seen (Hebrews 11:1). Faith in God is a very strong and complete source of hope and security that is known to man. Living by faith allows one to view life through the eyes of God and converge on the solution rather than the problem. We are also commanded not to walk or live by sight; the word *sight* comes from the Greek word *eidos*, which can be defined as things that appear or exist due in part to one's own reasoning ability. If one trusts in what he sees or understands solely by his *natural* reasoning abilities, already he has hindered his efforts of approaching and pleasing God, which can only occur by faith. "But without faith it is impossible to please him: for he that cometh to God must believe that he is, and that he is a rewarder of them that diligently seek him" (Hebrews 11:6). Once again, faith in God alone is the only means to achieve the Biblical promises of deliverance. Mankind should never have total faith in his own abilities to receive Biblical promises—particularly deliverance or freedom.

You can begin to experience miracles in your life simply by accepting or believing in the reality of God's promises of deliverance.

Changing Your Speech

If you've noticed, what we *say* plays a very important role in receiving the blessings of God. When we speak, we are generally acknowledging or agreeing to fact and truth. Even when people are not telling the truth, they are communicating what they desire to be of truth. Our words can actually *help* or *hinder*. For example, a young man who constantly confesses "I will never succeed in life due to my family's background [or my cultural history]" has already spoken *failure* and *defeat* on his life. Due to his negative thoughts, which will eventually manipulate and control the manner in which he believes, defeat and failure are certain to manifest or become evident in his life. Please listen carefully to the beginning of the next verse.

Proverbs 23:7a

7a. For as he thinketh in his heart, so is he.

There are two very important words that I must call attention to; they are *thinketh* and *heart*. I will begin with the word *thinketh*, which is derived from the Hebrew word *sha ʿar. Sha ʿar* is to allow an opening or create access to a place that is normally secured or protected: your mind, emotions, and will. Next is the word *heart*, which is derived from the Hebrew word *lev. Lev* is the innermost, deepest reigns of the soul (mind, emotions, and will) or the inner and immaterial nature of man. In other words, *lev* (*heart*) is the *life* of man. An interpretation of this verse could read: That which man gives access to his soul, he is certain to demonstrate or prove to be true. Your heart is very precious and dear to God, please guard what type of thoughts and ideas are allowed to enter into it. If your confession or declaration is "I am a recovering addict," it is vitally important that you discontinue making this statement. Please sever the relationship between yourself and the condition of addiction. The separation begins with a change in one's thoughts and speech. For example, when an individual accepts Jesus Christ as Lord and Savior, their confession is not "I am a recovering sinner." A sinner is someone who habitually sins or is disobedient to God's Word and is an unbeliever, which sharply contrasts someone who has accepted Jesus Christ as Lord and Savior and continues in his Word (St. John 8:31-32; 1 Timothy 1:15; 1 John 3: 4-10). Sin separates the individual from the presence of God and ultimately leads to eternal death, which is the "second" death (Revelation 2:11; 20:6,14). Separation from God is spiritual bondage, which reflects a life that's void of any communication and fellowship with God. Therefore, a Christian's testimony is "I am saved from the power and the curse of sin, and I am the righteousness of God in Christ Jesus" (Romans 6:2,7,12-14; 10:9-10,13). Although Christian's are physically unable to see God the Father, heaven, Jesus Christ, or the Holy Spirit, according to God's Word, through the faith that is within we have the ability to accept what God has to say about us and we have the assurance of knowing that we are no longer sinners. Please, begin saying what God says about you! Listen to what Peter wrote.

1 Peter 4:11

11. If any man speak, let him speak as the oracles of God; if any man minister, let him do it as of the ability which God giveth: that God in all things may be glorified through Jesus Christ, to whom be praise and dominion forever and ever. Amen.

We are commanded to "speak as the oracles of God" when we speak. Oracles are the wise and accurate sayings that are harmonious with the Word of God. To deliver, set free, or restore is one of the primary reasons God gave the holy scriptures to mankind. A vital component of Jesus's ministry was to preach *deliverance* to those who are held captive or are bound by the forces of darkness (Luke 4:18). But it doesn't end with preaching alone; listen to the next verse.

Colossians 1:12

12.Who [God the Father] hath delivered us from the power of darkness, and hath translated us into the kingdom of his dear Son.

Contrary to what the traditional message may be, every born-again Christian has been delivered, set free, or liberated from the power, authority, and strength of darkness. From previous Biblical examination, we understand the sins of witchcraft and sorcery are embraced in darkness. Therefore, if a Christian is once again entangled in the arena of darkness, it is solely due to yielding or relinquishing his authority and responsibility to remain free from temptations to enter into bondage or sin.

Begin and continue saying "I thank you God, my Father, for delivering me from the bondage of drug addiction and the power of sin" (inspired by St. John 8:32-36). After you have accepted Jesus Christ as Lord and Savior and begin speaking what God says about you, *deliverance* will begin to manifest itself in your life. Please listen to what Jesus Christ said in the Gospel according to Matthew.

Matthew 12:34b

34b. for out of the abundance of the heart [soul, mind] the mouth speaketh.

Everything that is in the heart (mind) will eventually be spoken out of the mouth. In other words, if I am bound, my speech will reflect that of a man who's life is in bondage; if I am free, my speech, of course, will reflect that of *free* or *delivered* man. Remember what we read in Proverbs 23:7a: "For as he thinketh in his heart, so is he." Once again, whatever one allows (whether it be positive or negative) to enter his soul and take root he will eventually imitate, and the validation of what has entered in will become evident by his speech. We shouldn't waste precious time confessing bondage or defeat to any condition that God has graciously provided freedom or liberation from. Let's read further and examine God's Word concerning our speech.

Proverbs 18:21

21. Death and life are in the power of the tongue: and they that love it shall eat the fruit thereof.

The Bible mentions a vehicle that helps to usher in death or life: the tongue. As most of us know death (spiritual and physical) is the result of sin and also a total separation from God. Therefore, we must understand that there is a separation between God and anything that is not agreeable with his character. Death is something God did not want to happen, and he takes no pleasure in it. "For I have no pleasure in the death of him that dieth, saith the Lord God: wherefore turn yourselves and live ye" (Ezekiel 18:32). Confessing or speaking "death," which is a work of darkness, is contrary to the character and will of God. Remember, death is the result of sin. Therefore, when you are speaking of yourself by saying "I" and associating the word *addiction* with it, you are speaking death upon yourself: "I am a recovering addict" or "I am an addict." The death that's being uttered is a spiritual bondage that is contrary to God's will for your life, and it will eventually lead to a premature physical death. I am not suggesting that you can physically kill yourself by merely speaking a word or group of words. The message I am conveying is people generally live what they speak. The Bible teaches that when speaking we are to speak as the oracles of God (1 Peter 4:11). The speech that is in harmony with the oracles of God allows one to look at a situation and call it what you desire it to become and never what it is. "And calleth those things which be not as though they were" (Romans 4:17).

The Hebrew equivalent to the word *life* is *chay*. Life, or chay, can be defined as alive, living, sustaining life, to be quickened, to return or restore from sickness, and adhering to the commandments or teachings of God. According to Deuteronomy 30:11-20, the choice between life and death is yours, and the final outcome is determined by either your obedience or disobedience to God's Word. When you speak life, say, for example "I thank you, Father, that not only have I been liberated from the bondage of drug addiction, but that I also live a life free of doubt." When you began to speak "life" over your condition, the thoughts of doubt, fear, and depression will begin to weaken. Once again, confessing God's Word over your condition will enable you to live a life of victory. God's Word simply replaces those negative and dark thoughts of bondage, such as "I am an addict" or "I am a recovering addict." Remember what we read in the Gospel according to John: "And you shall know the truth, and the truth shall make you free" (8:32), and "If the Son therefore shall make you free, you shall be free indeed" (8:36). There are two main reasons people continue to confess and label themselves recovering addicts *after* they have

67

come to God by way of Jesus Christ and have asked to be delivered from drug addiction. The first is a lack of knowledge of God's written Word, and the second is the reoccurrence of the temptations of drug use, which leads one to believe that he hasn't truly been delivered from the bondage of the illicit drug world. Please remember, the temptations *will* come. For example, if there was an undesirable guest in your house who wreaked havoc and all of a sudden you gained the power to evict him, at this point, the once undesirable guest would be standing outside, *pounding* on the door, hoping you will let him in again. The house is your body, the door is your heart (soul), and the poundings are the temptations of witchcraft and sorcery. One must remember that he is not categorized as an addict simply because he is bombarded with temptations to entertain a previous lifestyle he has been delivered from. Remember, you are the one who has the power or ability to allow or deny entrance of anything into your life again. These unclean spirits *will* return seeking to destroy the lives of those who have been delivered or cleansed (Matthew 12:43-45; 2 Peter 2:20-22). Proverbs 18:21 also says, "and they that love it shall eat the fruit thereof." The word *love* in the Hebrew language is pronounced *ahav*. To love is to have a close and strong emotional attachment to an object with a desire to possess the loved object. Therefore, if you love *life*, quite naturally you will speak life and ultimately experience the rewards or visible expressions of life. In contrast, if you love *death*, quite naturally you will speak or utter death and reap the rewards that death yields.

The sum of the matter is **it is impossible to speak death and reap life as much as it is impossible to speak life and reap death; WE WILL REAP WHAT WE SOW (Galatians 6:7-8).**

A healthy confession leads to a healthy life.

Reproving Negative Thoughts

A negative thought is an idea that is not positive or constructive and usually provokes one to develop an inferiority complex. Negative or contradicting thoughts normally arrive to combat the positive state of the psyche, which functions as the center of the thoughts, emotions, and behaviors of man. In other words, when you're feeling good and things are going well, negative thoughts and trouble usually appear to encourage a negative state of mind or character. According to St. Matthew 14:25-33, Jesus's disciples were in a ship on the sea, and Jesus went unto them walking on water. When Jesus's disciples saw him walking on water, they cried out for fear. "It is a spirit," Peter said, "Lord if it be thou, bid me come unto thee on the water." After Jesus said, "come," Peter began to walk on the water to go to Jesus. When Peter saw that the wind had become boisterous or unrestrained, immediately fear entered into Peter's heart and he began to sink. Jesus immediately stretched forth his hand and saved Peter and said, "O thou of little faith, wherefore didst thou doubt?" Peter had actually stepped out of a ship where everyone was surrounded by fear and began to walk toward victory. When fear and doubt (the wind) made its presence known, Peter took his eyes off of Jesus, who is our source of an abundant life (St. John 10:10) and he began to sink. The thought of sinking became reality in Peter's life because of his submission to the negative presence of fear. Jesus himself told Peter to come to him and Peter had begun to walk, until the thought of sinking entered his mind. Peter immediately forgot about the positive command of Jesus, which was to come (walk). I don't care if the devil himself walks up and tells you that you will always be an addict; rebuke the thought and KEEP YOUR EYES ON JESUS! Again, if Satan vigorously attacks you with the idea of "forever being an addict and never actually being totally delivered," immediately begin to rebuke that thought. To rebuke is to simply forbid and prove someone or something to be false or erroneous through careful evaluation. A proven method for achieving victory in one's life is to never confess the thoughts of Satan, which are always erroneous and negative. Paul wrote in his second epistle to the church at Corinth:

2 Corinthians 10:3-5

3. For though we walk in the flesh, we do not war after the flesh: 4.(For the weapons of our warfare are not carnal, but mighty through God to the pulling down of strongholds;)

5.Casting down imaginations, and every high thing that exalteth itself against the knowledge of God, and bringing into captivity every thought to the obedience of Christ.

Remember, the weapons that we use to fight Satan with are not carnal or fleshly. The weapons of a Christian are spiritual in nature and very powerful. Christians are equipped with a spiritual arsenal that has the ability to tear down and demolish any demonic force that tries to enslave God's people, especially those who have been liberated from strongholds in their lives. Strongholds are conditions or episodes of mental bondage in a person's life that utter the deceptive message of forever being bound—that there is no hope of true liberation. In other words, strongholds are spiritual chains with a spiritual padlock. In verse 4 of 2 Corinthians chapter 10, the Apostle Paul states, "For the weapons of our warfare are not carnal, but mighty through God." Attempting to confront Satan and his demonic regime with one's own ability or intellect is like going to battle without the proper training, body armor, and weapons. Spiritually, Christians are to confront circumstances and situations *after* seeking God's wisdom, ways, and instructions. Then, with great boldness, are they able to cast down all mental images (imaginations) and forms of reasoning that exalt itself against the knowledge and understanding of the Word of God. Imaginations are thoughts that intentionally oppose and demonstrate enmity toward the Word of God. In verse 5, the Apostle Paul states, "and bringing into captivity every thought to the obedience of Christ." The obedience of Christ is one's thought-life willingly becoming submissive to what is just or pleasing to God the Father. In other words, when your thoughts contradict what the Bible teaches concerning your life, it is your duty to see to it that your thoughts become harmonious with the message of the Bible. If you sincerely desire to be delivered from the bondage of drugs, began to view yourself as one who has been delivered and begin to confess your deliverance openly. Simply remember what God has done for all who have come to him by way of Jesus Christ. He *has* delivered us from the power of darkness (Colossians 1:13). Remember, whatever you speak and believe will eventually come to pass. With this principle there are two views to consider: good and evil. Ultimately you will have to decide whose depiction of your situation is worth listening to—God's or Satan's. You might have already noticed the most important element of being cured, delivered, or set free is a *relationship* with Jesus Christ. And it is also important to be mindful as to what you believe and say about yourself. Never hopelessly confess your problems to anyone, including yourself. If you must tell someone, talk to God. Once you have talked to God about your problem, leave it with him and then allow your Heavenly Father, by faith, to redirect your life. From that moment forward, be mindful of what you say or confess.

Thoughts are also known as the process and power of thinking, which are converted to a group of ideas. Those ideas, whether positive or negative, are spoken out of the mouth. The thoughts I am making reference to are the ideas people entertain and give life to. In other words, the thoughts one entertains will quite naturally be spoken out of the mouth. Usually, the continuous cycle of thinking and speaking, speaking and thinking, and thinking and speaking takes place. The aforementioned is a very common procedure used by millions of people to shape or direct their lives and future, whether positive or negative. They think and speak, speak and think; the process goes on and on. What most people do not understand is that, when one speaks, he is speaking to himself also, either positively or negatively. This process is explained in the next verse.

Proverbs 21:23

23. Whoso keepeth [guards] his mouth and his tongue keepeth [guards] his soul from troubles.

Remember, the *soul* is the mind, will, emotions, and intellect of man. Whosoever carefully manages or controls all that is spoken will build a spiritual fortress around one's mind (soul). The main reason people install fences or barriers around their property is to keep unwanted or uninvited guests from entering. Imagine installing a spiritual barrier around your mind (soul) to discontinue the entertainment of unfruitful

73

thoughts and eventually releasing these thoughts out of your mouth. Regardless of whether the words you have spoken are positive or negative, once you have spoken them, they have life. Ultimately these spoken words begin to shape your perception of people and events, particularly oneself. Once again, be mindful of what *you* have to say and think about yourself. If you know that you are a child of the living God and you have prayed to him for total deliverance from the bondage of the illicit drug world (witchcraft and sorcery), by faith receive his deliverance, walk in total victory, and only speak what your Heavenly Father says about you. Whenever Satan tempts you, be it the thought of reentering the illicit drug world or forever being an addict, remind him through words and actions that you are no longer under his control. Next, immediately begin to thank God for total deliverance from drug use and all other forms of illegal drug activity.

As you continue to march forward and experience the freedom that only God can give, Satan will attempt to attack you in the realm of your mind—mainly because Satan and all other demonic spirits cannot possess the body of a born-again Christian (2 Corinthians 10:3-5; 1 Corinthians 3:16; 1 John 4:4). To remain victorious, it is important that you read and study the Bible on a daily basis, constantly communicate with God through prayer, and become a member of a wholesome Bible-teaching ministry. And most importantly, one should also pursue a lifestyle that is free of sin. Satan's greatest method of defeating people is luring them into a lifestyle of sin and destroying them with the sin of that lifestyle. As Christians, we have many warnings and examples in the Bible pertaining to the schemes and methods used by Satan to destroy the lives of mankind. Remember, victory begins with how and what *you* believe about yourself.

Healthy thoughts lead to healthy lives.

Feasting on the Word of God

According to the Bible, the fashion of man is spirit, soul, and body (1 Thessalonians 5:23). Just as natural food is nourishment for our natural bodies, so is the Bible to our born-again spiritual bodies. In reference to our natural bodies, a healthy diet provides sufficient energy, essential acids, and vitamins and minerals to support desired growth. If there is an absence of essential nutrients or food altogether, malnutrition will result. Quite amazingly, the aforementioned process is very similar to the spiritual growth of Christians. With disciplined study habits, one will grow to spiritual maturity and quite naturally fulfill or satisfy the purpose for which he or she was born. Whenever there is an absence of a proper spiritual diet or study life, spiritual malnutrition will result and one will not be able to stand against or discern the schemes of Satan. The choice is totally yours: Choose to study, which leads to spiritual maturity, or become passive in the studying of the holy scriptures, which will eventually lead to spiritual malnutrition. Let's explore a few passages in which we are instructed to study and live by God's Word.

Matthew 4:3-4

3. And when the tempter [Satan] came to him [Jesus], he said, If thou be the Son of God command that these stones be made bread.

4. But he [Jesus] answered and said, It is written, Man shall not live by bread alone, but by every word that proceedeth out of the mouth of God.

This is an account of one of three occasions when Satan tempted Jesus in the wilderness. To tempt someone is to test the person's will and solicit sin. First and most importantly, Satan *knew* that Jesus was the Son of God. Satan directed his temptations toward Jesus to tempt him to turn the stones into bread, satisfy his natural appetite, and obey Satan's commands. Remember, Satan knows that all Christians have been set free. Otherwise, there wouldn't be a need to bring an onslaught of temptations by way of people and unhealthy thoughts or desires. Jesus had fasted for forty days. Quite naturally, his physical body was hungry and craved natural food. Satan, being the deceiver that he is, immediately attacked the natural appetite of Jesus by tempting Jesus to turn the stones into bread to satisfy the natural yearning for food. Yes, Jesus needed and wanted to eat, but he was teaching mankind a valuable lesson of not allowing Satan to tempt you to do anything, even if it seems natural or harmless. Anything Satan does or presents has a hidden price associated with it: death, destruction, or embarrassment. Jesus immediately quotes a portion of Deuteronomy 8:3 to convey the message to Satan that he will live by or follow all the commands of Almighty God (see 2 Timothy 3:16-17 also). Peter wrote:

1 Peter 2:2

2. As newborn babes, desire the sincere milk of the word, that ye may grow thereby.

As previously stated, natural foods are composed of the essential nutrients necessary to sustain life as well as to promote physical growth. In a remarkably similar manner, the Bible, when read on a consistent basis, will produce spiritual nutrients such as wisdom, holiness, power, and protection. As you continue to feed your spirit on the awesome and powerful Word of the living God, you will begin to notice that your soul (mind, emotions, will, and life) is being enlightened and transformed. Paul wrote:

Romans 12:2

2. And be not conformed to this world: but be ye transformed by the renewing of your mind, that you may prove what is that good, and acceptable, and perfect will of God.

We are urged not to *conform* or succumb to the external and destructive ways of this world or society, as we understand it to be. This does not mean that we are not to obey the laws of our government officials; I am merely stating that we are in this world, but our character should not portray the sinful behavior that has manifested itself through the manner of life depicted by society. Your transformation from darkness to the light, which must begin in your mind (soul), is initiated when you are saved, or born again. Regardless of the thoughts and ways of popular society, you must remember you are undergoing a marvelous change or renovation and there is no time to be squandered. Understand that mankind is physically strong in stature, however, the body will always yield to the desires of your mind, whether its good or bad, healthy or unhealthy, or freedom or bondage. As you continue to nourish your soul with the Word of God, you will acquire strength to boldly and successfully confront the lusts or unhealthy desires of the flesh. The Bible is your sword; therefore, use it like a mighty warrior. Hebrews chapter four states:

Hebrews 4:12

12. For the word of God is quick, and powerful, and sharper than any two-edged sword, piercing even to the dividing asunder of soul and spirit, and of the joints and marrow, and is a discerner of the thoughts and intents of the heart.

We have used the Word of God to better understand the subject of drug use and drug solicitation. We have also used the Word of God to examine the *cause*, the *effect*, and the *cure* of illegal drug activity. By recognizing that addiction occurs as part of a process, we also understand that the only weapon sharp enough to cut through the forces that govern this form of behavior is the Word of God. By recognizing or exposing the forces responsible for this negative behavior, we are able to penetrate the darkness and introduce God's marvelous light (the Bible), which imparts hope to what appears to be a hopeless situation. Please understand a common mistake made in the unveiling of darkness is attempting to identify the glorious truths of God while living a life of total darkness, or without the aid of Jesus Christ. This is exactly what millions of people are doing today, and as a result, they have become weary in trying to resolve or cure an unwanted condition such as drug addiction, which has a very devastating affect on an individual's life. In other words, many are superficially attempting to understand the spiritual process involved in illicit drug use. It is impossible to understand the spiritual truths of God solely through the use of the natural or carnal mind. The Bible is a mighty weapon, and when properly employed it becomes a double-edged sword that gives life, direction, purpose, and sound judgment. For example, in times of temptation, man can follow the example of Jesus in

Matthew 4:4: "But he answered and said, It is written." In other words, allow the Bible to give the final verdict. In addition, please examine the following passage from the Psalms.

Psalms 1:1-3

1.Blessed is the man that walketh not in the counsel of the ungodly, nor standeth in the way of sinners, nor sitteth in the seat of the scornful.

2.But his delight is in the law of the Lord; and in his law doth he meditate day and night.

3.And he shall be like a tree planted by the rivers of water, that bringeth forth his fruit in his season; his leaf also shall not wither; and whatsoever he doeth shall prosper.

For those who desire to become blessed or happy is usually dependent upon them not heeding the advice and guidance of those whose morals, according to the God's teachings, are considered immoral. Furthermore, your happiness (blessedness) will also be dependent upon your ability to not model your way of life after anyone who habitually sins and is a despiser of those who lead a life that's spiritually and morally upright. In addition, pursue a lifestyle that's fueled or motivated by the desire to meditate throughout the course of the day on the Word of God. To meditate simply means to reflect on or to consider during active thought processes, sometimes in a low, indistinct utterance (Joshua 1:8;

Psalms 1:1-3). With diligent compliance to the Bible's basic instructions, one will soon notice his life gradually making a change toward prosperity. The evidence of a Christian living prosperously is experiencing success or favor spiritually, mentally, physically, and/or financially.

Remember, God also gave us the Bible to teach and correct what is considered an unfitting or improper way of living and provide true guidance, which leads to a healthy and suitable life. In addition, the Bible is the only weapon (other than prayer) that Christians have to combat the wiles of Satan. The power of God's Word operating in mankind hinges upon one accepting and believing the truth of his unchanged doctrine. Jesus Christ *is* the Lamb of God who was slain for the sin of mankind (St. John 1:29).

According to Romans 3:23, "For all have sinned, and come short of the glory of God." The glory referred to here is the perfect, spiritually mature and whole state of man which allows him to have constant unbroken fellowship with God. Glory also gives man complete dominion over the Earth and all demonic forces (Genesis 1:26-28; St. Luke 10:19). If you desire to become one of his children (St. John 1:12) and live in God's fullness, simply acknowledge that you're a sinner in need of a savior or deliverer and repent (turn away from) of your sins.

This can be accomplished by praying this prayer:

"Dear God, I come to you in the awesome name of Jesus Christ. I acknowledge that I am a sinner and I am sorry for sinning against you. God, according to your Word, You said that, if I should call upon the name of the Lord, I would be saved. You said that, if I would declare that Jesus Christ is Lord and believe in my heart that you raised Jesus from the dead, I would be saved. Right now, before heaven and before man, I confess and acknowledge Jesus Christ as Lord and Savior of my life. Jesus, I open my heart to you, and I close my life to the things that are sinful to you. I thank you, Jesus, for saving and cleansing me of all sin and unrighteousness. I love you, Lord. Please lead me to a healthy, well-balanced church so that I may grow to become a mature Christian. Amen.

If you prayed this prayer, you are now saved, regenerated, or born again! If the devil or anyone else attempts to tell you anything contrary, simply stand firm on God's unchanged Word as it is written in St. John 1:12; 3:16; 6:47; 14:6; Acts 2:21; and

Romans 5:6-11; 10:9-10,13. May God bless you today and forevermore. Amen.

Glossary of Terms

Addict - an individual who is compulsively and physiologically dependent on a habit-forming substance or activity

Analgesic - a medicine ingested for the purpose of reducing or eliminating pain throughout the body

Anesthetic - a drug that produces anesthesia, which is a loss of sensation (feeling) with or without a loss of consciousness

Children of disobedience - those who have careless attitude and are obstinate in their way of living, especially in their rejection to the will of God

Coca - an Andean evergreen shrub with leaves that contain cocaine

Euphoria - a feeling of great happiness or well being

Flee - run away, shun, vanish, or escape.

Fool - an individual who lacks commonsense perception of the reality of things natural or spiritual (W. E. Vines)

Hallucination - a false or distorted perception of objects or events with a compelling sense of their reality

Neurotransmitter - a substance that transmits nerve impulses across a synapse

Resist - remaining firmly against; to oppose

Stupor - a state of reduced sensibility and mental numbness; daze

Submit - to yield or be under the obedience of the will or authority of another

Synapse - the junction between two communicating neurons

Synthetic - not natural or genuine; artificial

About the Author

Murray Miller, as a young man, dedicated his life to the Lord Jesus Christ. He immediately understood the importance of becoming a student of the Bible and embarked upon an expository study of God's Word. Today, Murray serves as a Bible and Life Skills instructor to those who are confronted with many of life's challenges. The majority of his work has been administered within churches and the local jails and prisons. He holds a Bachelor of Science degree from High Point University and is dedicated to teaching the Word of God in an inspiring, comprehensive and applicable manner.

www.ingramcontent.com/pod-product-compliance
Lightning Source LLC
Chambersburg PA
CBHW031258280526
45784CB00004B/1895